Airport

Byron Barton

Thomas Y. Crowell   New York

Copyright © 1982 by Byron Barton. All rights reserved.
Printed in the United States of America. No part of this
book may be used or reproduced in any manner
whatsoever without written permission except in the case
of brief quotations embodied in critical articles and
reviews. For information address Thomas Y. Crowell
Junior Books, 10 East 53rd Street, New York, N.Y. 10022.
Published simultaneously in Canada by Fitzhenry &
Whiteside Limited, Toronto.
Library of Congress Cataloging in Publication Data
Barton, Byron. Airport. Summary: Describes and pictures
what happens from the time an airplane passenger arrives
at an airport and boards an airplane until the plane is in
the air.   1. Airports—Juvenile literature. [1. Airports]
I. Title. TL725.B33 1982   387.7'36   79-7816 AACR2
·ISBN 0-690-04168-3 ISBN 0-690-04169-1 (lib. bdg.)
First Edition

In buses

and in cars

people come to the airport.

They come to fly

in big jet planes.

Gate 6 ➡

In the waiting room

they sit and wait

while outside their planes

get loaded and checked.

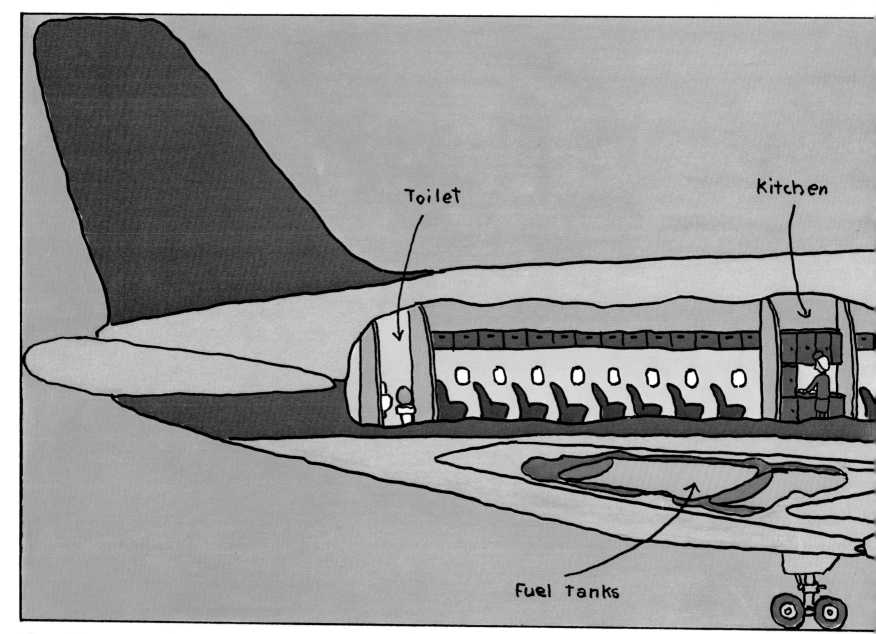

Suitcases go into the cargo hold.

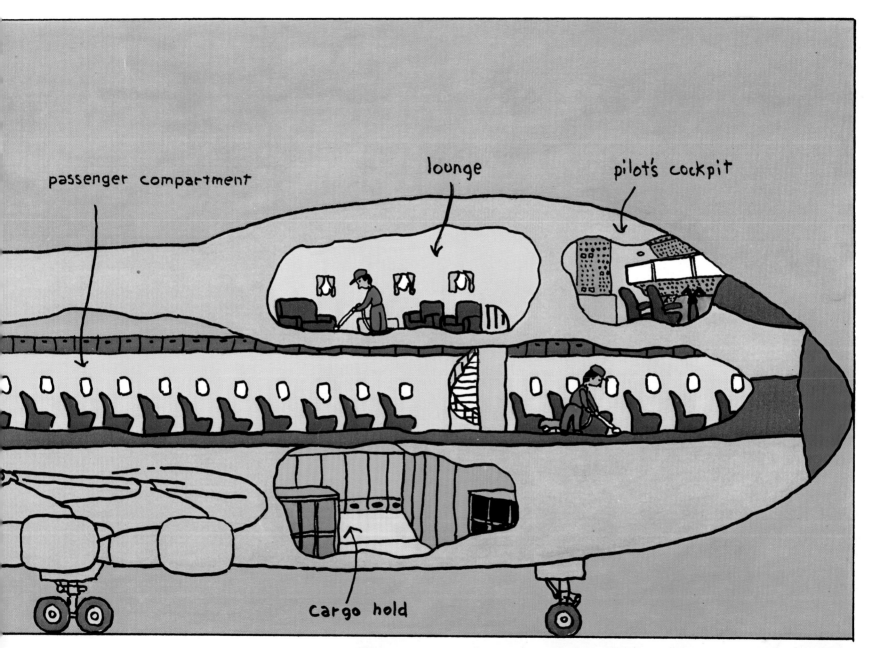

Fuel goes inside the wings.

Then the people

go on board.

They go inside

and find their seats.

Up front in the cockpit

the pilots get ready.

The control tower radios

when all is clear.

Buckle your seatbelts,

the stewardess says.

The big plane starts rolling

slowly to the runway.

Control tower to pilot:

All clear for takeoff.

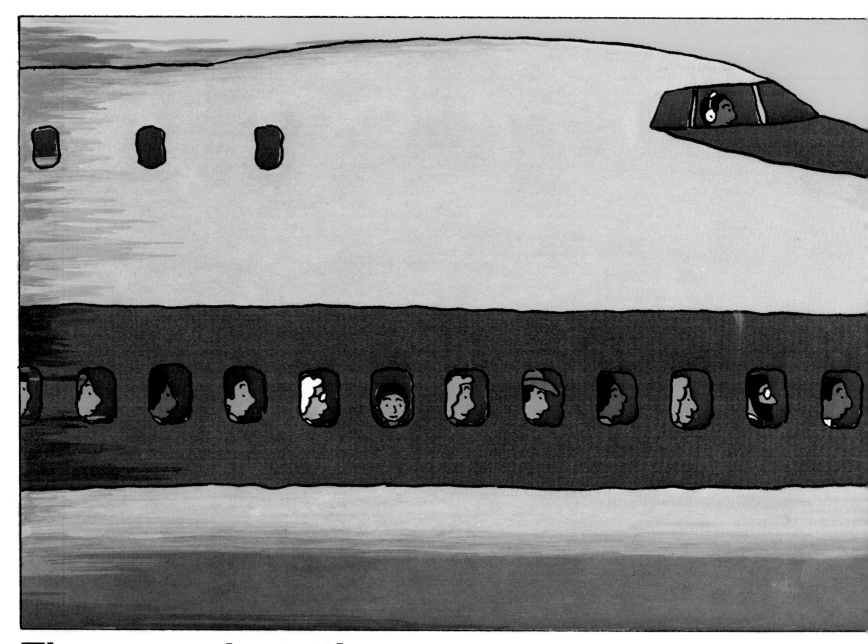

They roar down the runway

faster and faster,

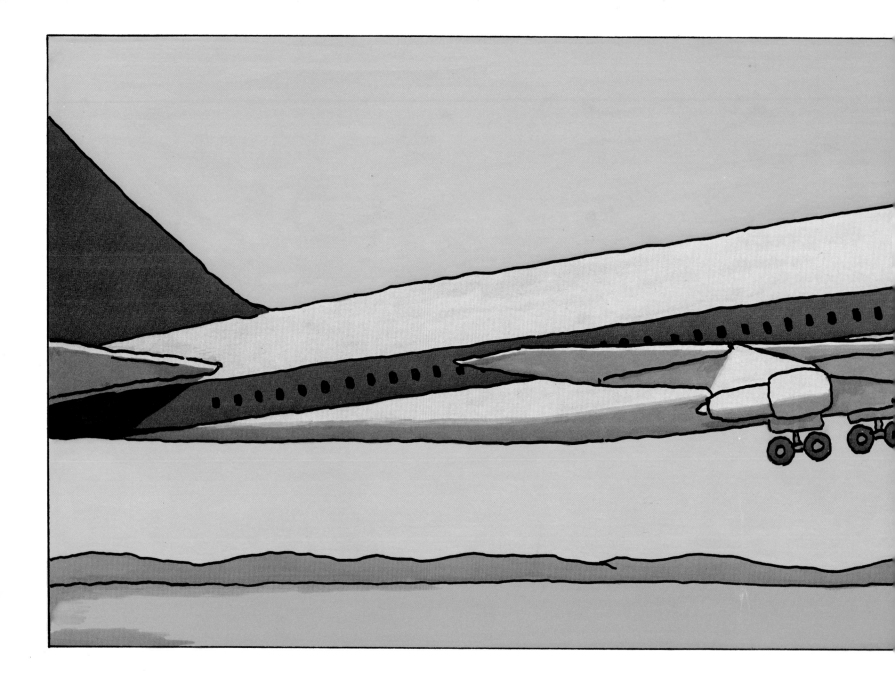

then up in the air.

They are on their way.